The secret to saving marriage

King Shegz

Contents

Foreword

It is most helpful to have some kind of manual to help couples finish their journey without the bumps and scratches they usually bring. However, it is very popular to say that most people learn from their own experience or the experience of others.

INTENTIONALLY LEFT BLANK

Chapter 1:

Basics Of Relationship

Summary

The incompatibility factor is one of the main causes of problems in marital relationships. After the initial excitement of the new relationship wears off, the couple soon find themselves trapped in a situation they have nothing in common with. This can be a positive thing if handled well, but it often leads to a lot of negativity in the equation and ultimately to a marriage breakdown.

Basic Information

To be able to ensure that the relationship has a better chance of surviving; Both parties need to question their roles and perceptions of the relationship. You should discuss compatibility, understanding, cooperation, similar interests, types of interests, points of disagreement and pleasure, and anything else that may dictate your type of participation. Either party will prolong the relationship. When it comes to the negative side of a relationship, both parties need to be acutely aware of how to handle these situations and how long the negativity lasts until a resolution is reached. It is also important to consider how to find and combine these solutions in an effort to get the relationship back on track. These questions are worth exploring early in the relationship, as they are helpful in guiding the future course of the relationship. It's also a good way to gauge the potential for continuing that particular relationship and what the end goal is expected.

INTENTIONALLY LEFT BLANK

Chapter 2:
Plan Time Together

Summary

For a relationship to work, both parties need to be equally committed to making the relationship as good as possible. This includes discovering ways to spend time together without being forced.

Enjoy Each Other's Company

Trying to make time for each other is very important if a couple intends to develop the relationship and keep it happy and healthy for the long term. Without making an effort to spend quality time together, the couple can break up and this can even lead to the possibility of divorce. Spending time together is especially important, especially when you both have busy and hectic work lives. When this happens, it's easy to use work and other distractions as an excuse not to spend time together. This is of course a very bad habit to have in a relationship.

Here are some suggestions on how to create the perfect foundation to spend quality time together to keep a relationship current and strong:

• By the time the relationship reaches its current stage, both parties will be doing things together that are interesting enough to consider taking the next step in building the relationship. So, trying to continue to engage in similar activities will benefit the relationship.

• Finding new things to do together that both parties will enjoy is another good way to create opportunities to spend time together as a couple. These new activities should ideally be a form that both parties will enjoy, but sometimes it may be necessary to indulge in something that only one of the partners really enjoys.

INTENTIONALLY LEFT BLANK

Chapter 3:
Use Love Letters And Date Nights

Summary

When it comes to keeping a relationship vibrant and exciting, it's often necessary to spice things up once in a while. This can be done using love letters or it can be an overnight date.

How to show your care

In the early stages of a new relationship, these two activities are much practiced and even expected. Unfortunately, however, as the relationship progresses to a more familiar stage, both parties can begin to take each other for granted and one of the most common ways for awareness to become apparent in a relationship is lack of love letters and dating. Most people make the mistake of thinking that such sex is no longer necessary or unnecessary, thus falling into a rather boring routine that will eventually lead to a troubled relationship. Couples who do not pursue these activities as the relationship progresses, the risks are obvious, and when there are outside opportunities, there is always the possibility of being tempted by these temptations, so they will seek justification for that infatuation. So in the quest to not only keep the relationship as exciting as it was in the beginning, the couple should continue to exchange love letters and date to ensure that there is no temptation to seek out such activities in other places. Actively participating in activities will also keep the couple looking forward to those lovely moments and will also ensure that both parties stay committed to doing their best. This will include both the physical and emotional aspects of the relationship.

INTENTIONALLY LEFT BLANK

Chapter 4:
Maintain Physical And Mental Health

Summary

During the dating phase, everyone usually goes the extra mile to look their best and most attractive. Unfortunately, this is not the case as the couple becomes comfortable with each other and has been in love for a while. Experts in this field especially recommend not to neglect appearance. The same is true when it comes to an individual's spiritual growth in a committed relationship.

Show Pride In Yourself

People don't seem to understand the importance of following these two fronts. Neither party is interested in returning home to a relationship where no effort is made to keep the other party excited and guessing. Boredom is often the result of that disinterest, and it will eventually force both parties to seek excitement outside of the existing relationship. There is always the risk that the partner at home is the last to let his appearance and physical condition deteriorate. Some people just don't seem to understand the impact they have on others with a complete lack of regard for overall upkeep, both mentally and physically. This especially happens when there are so many temptations outside of the marriage cycle, it often prompts the losing side of exactly what they are lacking. It is also one of the main reasons why the relationship has endured a time of infidelity and discord. Busy schedules and commitments are often the reason for a lack of focus on keeping yourself in top shape, both mentally and physically. If both parties aren't making a concerted effort to look good to each other, then you're definitely underestimating the relationship.

Chapter 5:
Put Your Spouse At The Top Of The List

Summary

Making a spouse feel important and loved in a relationship is sure to benefit both parties, as the effort put in will go unnoticed in the long run. Making someone feel important is not only a fun way to show love and respect for that person, but also another way to cherish a loved one.

Put them on the pedestal

Happy couples will almost always attest that treating each other with respect and love helps in keeping the relationship strong and standing the test of time. In addition to more obvious reasons such as love and respect for the spouse, this treatment will also reveal how much value an individual places on the existence of the spouse in the context of the relationship generation. It would also be a very natural reciprocal action to return from the receiving party, thus making the relationship even stronger and longer lasting. The most common way to develop a mate-first attitude in thought and action is to always consult with your spouse when making important decisions that may affect your partner. . Others may include finding ways to keep your spouse happy and satisfied in the relationship, making a conscious effort to indulge, or organizing activities that make your spouse feel special and loved. , even buying small gifts for no particular reason, except to express love. Simple actions that don't have much to do with work or money, like opening a door or pulling a chair for a spouse, will help a spouse feel special and loved. Always choosing to spend quality time with your mate whenever the opportunity arises is also one way to put your spouse at the top of the list

INTENTIONALLY LEFT BLANK

CHAPTER 6:

The Essence Of Saving A Marriage

Summary

Marriage is not something to be taken lightly and even more so when there are signs in the relationship that indicate some degree of difficulty. Most people try to take the necessary steps to save the marriage before giving up or raising the white flag in case of failure.

Don't Quit!

Every marriage is worth saving, and it certainly is worth the effort to save what was once something beautiful and wonderful. Exercise is even more important if children are involved. Here are a few ways to find out if both parties really want to save the marriage:

- Take time to talk about the things that ruined the marriage. This may not be easy to do without outside help such as a support group or counseling sessions. Attempting to do so without guidance could lead to an argument between the couple or worse, a heated match in which baseless accusations would escalate the situation.
- Really looking for another opportunity to make the marriage work is another option to explore in your quest to save the marriage. Sometimes asking for another chance and then taking all the necessary steps to ensure sincere effort is being made will help both parties see marriage in a different light. Actively participating in the ultimate goal of saving a marriage will require commitment and persistence.

CONCLUSION

There's really no point in giving up on a marriage that's wasted years and lots of work. As long as there's still love in the picture, there's still a chance to make things happen. However, it's important to know when a relationship ends for the better, such as toxic or abusive situations. If the spark is still there, you should definitely try some of the tips above to fix your marriage, after some people think you only have one true love.

www.ingramcontent.com/pod-product-compliance
Lightning Source LLC
LaVergne TN
LVHW020545160826
845677LV00015B/4220

* 9 7 9 8 8 4 7 2 6 9 4 4 5 *